SURFING OREGON

SURFING OREGON

Second Edition By Michael Botkins

Published By

 Clean and Green Enterprises LLC
Portland, Oregon

The author and publisher herby disclaim any liability to any party for any loss or damage caused by errors or omissions within this publication.

ISBN 978-0-6151-4498-6

Printed in The United States of America

Please direct suggestions, comments, or questions to:
cleanandgreenent@yahoo.com

Special Thanks to Contributing Photographers

Jeremy & Marney Starkey
www.dblvizion.com
808.205.7220
Central Oregon Coast

Table of Contents

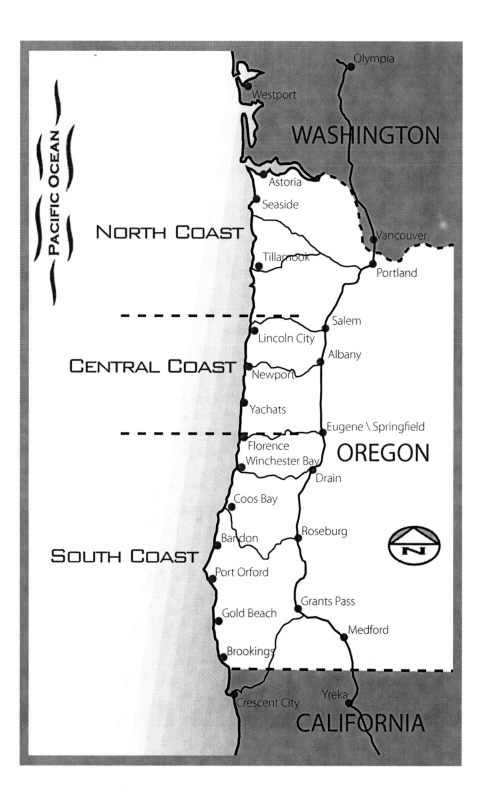

INTRODUCTION

OK, first things first. Oregon has some great surf and always has, naturally it's always had surfers to reap the harvest. Don't worry guys and gals, this guide is only intended to introduce the beginning surfer or recent Oregon transplant to surfing in Oregon, your secret spots are not on the list. All the information in this guide is available elsewhere, I've simply compiled it. If you've been surfing in Oregon for at least 5 or 10 years its quite obvious that surfing is becoming exponentially popular in the Northwest, as well as worldwide. This guide will hopefully help everybody branch out from the few ultra-crowded spots and seek the treasures that Oregon has to offer.

I should also mention at this point that this is a surf guide only. I considered locating public and private campgrounds as well as hotels and eateries on the maps but there are simply too many, they would be a guide among themselves. Just take a look around, you won't be disappointed at what you find. I recommend that you pick up a travel guide for places to eat and sleep on the Oregon coast, as well as other tourist attractions (for flat days of course).

One day when I was bailing my work early to go surf a co-worker said "surf's up eh?", and I said "actually its finally down". Or neighbors have commented on how calm the ocean is and how I must be praying for surf, when actually there was good fun swell out there. Later I thought that just about sums up surfing in Oregon. Unlike most places there's almost always swell, in fact there's often too much of it and it touches on the point of how accustomed we are in the NW (surfers and regular folk alike) to the powerful Pacific and our proximity to the weather systems that send waves across the globe.

That being said, Oregon, just like any coastal area, has it's day, and Oregon definitely gets its share of them. For those who are dedicated and motivated to hike the extra mile or two, golden era surfing experiences abound.

© Cove Photo

GEOGRAPHY

The Oregon coast is normally broken into three regions; 1) **North Coast:** Columbia River to Cascade Head, 2) **Central Coast:** Cascade Head to Florence, and 3) **South Coast:** Florence to Brookings / California Border. The North Coast ("crown jewel") area has the most surf spots mile for mile, some of the most consistently good conditions and subsequently the largest crowds. The latter because of its proximity to Portland and other large valley metropolitan areas. The Central ("red headed step child") and South ("last frontier") Coasts are less populated with more fickle surf conditions, especially during the summer when North winds can be fierce and blow unabated for weeks on end. This guide will follow the above described breakdown.

© DoubleVizion

SURFING IN OREGON

The majority of surf spots in Oregon are beach breaks, so naturally the quality depends not only on ocean conditions but the sand as well. This opens up literally hundreds of miles of empty beaches just begging for a go-out. As mentioned before there is often an abundance of swell, so what looks like fun beach break surf from a hilltop may in actuality be a **duck-dive** nightmare. So naturally we look for ways to slip out, namely rocky headland or jetties that partially block swell and provide a route to the outside breakers. These same obstructions can help reduce or redirect wind in a favorable manner. Find rock points or jetties in Oregon and you'll find surfers.

Oregon also has its share of **point / reef** waves but tragically not nearly as many as one would think when considering a map of the coast line.

CLIMATE AND SEASONS

Because of the giant Pacific Ocean and the cool California Current that sweeps the entire coast, Oregon coastal areas have very moderate weather. Air temps in the summers usually peak around 70°F while winter nights rarely dip below 40°F. It should be noted that it can get extremely hot during periods of summer Chinook Winds (Oregon's version of Santa Ana Winds) and inversely chilly during winter cold snaps (which usually coincide with excellent surf conditions).

Generally speaking, summer has quite reliable Northerly (from the North) winds which are usually light and variable in the mornings and often quite strong in the afternoon. Summer surfing in Oregon is mostly beach break **windswell**, peaky and fun. Occasional strong Southern Hemisphere, long interval **groundswells** make their way to Oregon during the summer months, providing fun surf at Southern exposures for those patient enough to sit and wait for inconsistent sets. Incredible to think that these waves have traveled upwards of 8,000 miles on their way to our coast.

Winter low pressure storm systems bring mostly Southerly winds which can be intense at times, turning the ocean into a boiling and deadly froth. BUT, when those same lows slip to the South, East winds blow, clearing and calming the ocean, and the Oregon coast comes alive with world class surf!

© Cove Photo

Spring and fall are transition seasons. In the fall the North winds are slackening and an early storm is possible. While in spring the weather is clearing and the high pressure born Northerlies are just starting to crank up. Arguably most Oregon surfers would agree that fall is the best season for surf. Certainly it's the best general weather season on the coast (ie: good surf conditions) with some early lows forming in the North Central Pacific and Gulf of Alaska, sending some ideal groundswell in our direction.

Great waves can be found in Oregon on any given day in any given season, but that's just it, they must be found. You're not going to check a web cam or call a surf shop and be guaranteed good surf with a little drive down the street. Explore and discover and you will be amply rewarded for your efforts.

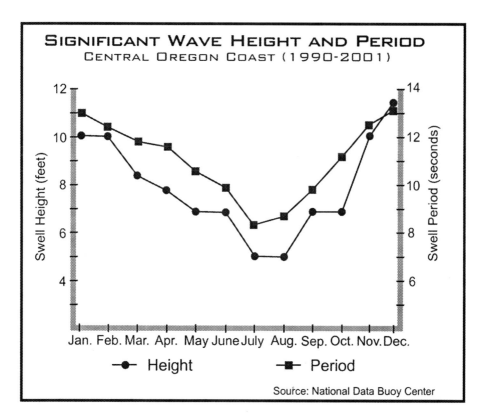

SIGNIFICANT WAVE HEIGHT AND PERIOD
CENTRAL OREGON COAST (1990-2001)

Source: National Data Buoy Center

SWELL AND SURF

Most surfing in Oregon is done on windswell waves which are usually **peaky** and consistent, perfect for beach break. Groundswells are less frequent but far from rare, occurring mostly in the fall and winter. Travelling much greater distances, these swells are much more organized (ie: lines and **walls**) and usually have defined **"sets** and **lulls"**. On Oregon's coast we can see groundswells created relatively nearby in the North Pacific (borderline windswells) and others that were born in the Southern Hemisphere out of the Antarctic. Few places can hold much larger than double overhead surf without serious loss of quality and shape. Subsequently much of the coast is considered unsurfable during periods of winter. Not to worry though, Oregon waves pack plenty of power for their size.

BOARDS

Generally speaking surfboards for the Northwest are a bit longer, wider, thicker, and more heavily glassed then their warm water cousins. These specs seem to suit the windy conditions and heavily rubberized surfer in the cold water waves of Oregon.

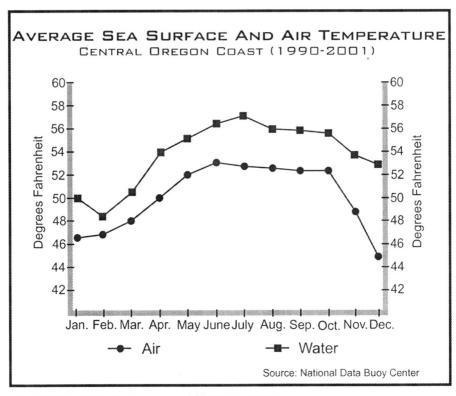

Average Sea Surface And Air Temperature
Central Oregon Coast (1990-2001)

Source: National Data Buoy Center

Water Temps and Wetsuits

Most people shrivel (literally) when they consider stepping into the icy North Pacific, and rightfully so, the water can get downright frigid in Oregon. However they are usually surprised to hear about the range in seasonal water temps. Adding to that, phenomenon such as "el Nino" can bring Oregon water temps up to the pleasant \ trunkable range. While prolonged periods of Northerly flow or "Chinook Winds" (hard offshores) can pull values down into the frigid department (is that ice forming on my eyelids?). Keep in mind that the chart above shows average water temperatures and doesn't really reflect the daily or weekly fluctuations that can occur due to several variables such as those mentioned above. For me the coldest water I've felt was in July after a couple weeks of hard Northerly winds. I think most Oregonians would agree that the water feels the coldest during the summer, relative to air temperature anyway.

Normally a **5-4-3** wetsuit is the standard apparel for Oregon waters, with booties and attached hood. Gloves are optional and worn by about half of the population. Suits on either side of this standard are regularly worn, a 4-3 for the heartier folk on "warmer" days or a 6-4-3 for the reptilian kind (me).

Water quality on the Oregon Coast is generally good to excellent, when pollution levels do reach the advisory zone or closings occur they are listed on the Oregon Surf Page and the State of Oregon website (see Internet Resources).

WAX

Shocker here, use cold water wax. Base coat is nice also. Here's a little tip: if its in the 40's or below outside on the way to your go-out, keep the wax up front with you in the car, on the dash or something or even in your pocket. That'll keep it semi soft, so it doesn't feel like a piece of granite when you try to wax your board. Oh yeah, don't leave it on the dash of your car while you're out surfing.

© Cove Photo

SHARKS

Hey, it's the ocean, they're out there. I've seen a few big fish and people get bumped occasionally or even bit (rarely with life threatening injuries). The only regular practiced precaution that I know of with concern to sharks is to avoid surfing near river mouths when there is a salmon run happening (salmon = seals = sharks). Fin cuts or crossing Hwy 101 is more likely to cause you bodily harm, I think. If you're interested in learning more about sharks on the Pacific coast, reporting an incident, or simply getting spooked, check out the Shark Research Committee (see Internet Resources).

© Botkins

ETHICS

Now is a great opportunity to make a statement about the rules of engagement when surfing with other humans, especially strangers.

Rule 1) Safety, surfing is dangerous, don't do anything that will unnecessarily endanger you or anyone around you.

Rule 2) Always aid fellow surfers in need.

Rule 3) Know your surfing ability and attitude, choose where you surf accordingly.

Rule 4) When paddling back out to the line-up, yield right-of-way to on-coming surfers.

Rule 5) Wait your turn! Don't back paddle, if you've just caught a wave (or even just paddled for and missed one), it's someone else's turn, hang on the **inside** for a while.

Rule 6) The deeper surfer or closest to the peak has priority on the wave, take a look before you go.

Rule 7) Think before you paddle out. How would you feel if your solo beach break session was fouled by four or five aggressive bros? Travel light.

ACCESS

Access and parking in Oregon are generally abundant in the places where the road is near the beach. Other places require varying lengths of hiking to get to the water. These places seem to be the most rewarding because of the little extra effort. Remember that the beach (from the vegetation line to the sea) in Oregon is public property, access to it may be somewhat restricted but once you're there no one can restrict your presence. Access is protected under two separate pieces of legislation maintained by the Oregon Department of Parks and Recreation; 1) The Oregon Beach Bill of 1967 and 2) State Planning Goal 17 for Shorelands. There have been legal disputes about this in the past, for more info and some light reading check out Oregon Revised Statutes 390.605-755, you'll get right on that I know.

US HIGHWAY 101

The Pacific Coast Highway (US101) is the main access route on the Oregon coast and runs a total of 363 miles from the Columbia River South to the California Border. Mile-post markers start at zero in the North and increase as you drive Southward. At times it skirts the beaches and cliffs providing incredible panoramas, but more often than not (especially on the North coast) its just out of sight from the ocean or even several miles inland. This underscores the importance of a good map (Delorme Gazetteer) because most of the side roads that reach the coast are poorly marked as coastal access routes.

CAMPING ON THE OREGON COAST

State and local county parks as well as private campgrounds and RV parks litter the Oregon coast, (see Internet Resources). All of these facilities are usually very busy or full during the summer months so planning ahead (tough I know) is a good idea. The state campgrounds will usually hang a "Campground Full" sign out by the highway when there are no spots available. Off season periods find these campgrounds very sparsely populated and tranquil. Other options for the budget minded and camper equipped are pullouts right off Highway 101. They're everywhere and it's legal to crash for a night or two, just stay low key and you will be left alone. Also, logging roads are abundant and with some exploration sweet little spots can be found. The down side is the possibility of being roused in the night by the occasional timber cruiser or enraged meth head. Trust me, laying out 15 bucks for a site at the county park seems pretty reasonable at that point.

THE QUICK CHECK FORMAT

For all the spots listed in this guide I've used a standardized "Quick Check" format to give the basics of the spot, then in the "Notes" section I give some particulars that are unique to each spot. Next is a sample "Quick Check" with some examples of the descriptors you may encounter in one.

 Quick Check

> *Type of Wave*: **point, reef, exposed beach, protected beach, bay or river wave**
> *Power*: **mushy \ beginner, fun, juicy, explosive**
> *Swell Size and Direction*: **groundswell, windswell**, size is given in face feet, direction is where the swell is coming from
> *Wind Direction*: direction the wind is coming from
> *Tide*: level of tide that is best suited but not exclusive to a particular spot
> *Crowd Factor*: empty to ultra crowded and everywhere in between
> *Access*: parking, hiking, etc…, maybe directions if applicable
> *Hazards*: rocks, **rips**, sharks, etc…(pretty much every spot)
> *Vibe*: general atmosphere in the water (what to expect)

Notes: anything else, specific details

Terms

Here is a list of the **bold faced** words used in this guide that may need a little more explanation.

windswell- Locally generated (less than about 500 miles) swell with a period of about 11 seconds or less. Generally pretty consistent, ie: waves breaking constantly without much break or lull in between.

groundswell- Swell that has traveled a significant distance and have a period above 11 seconds. Tend to be more organized with obvious swell lines and distinct sets and lulls.

period \ interval- Elapsed time, in seconds, between peaks of waves.

peaky- Term used to describe tight, short breaking and peeling waves, common with windswell.

walls- Long swell lines associated with longer interval swells, unless they come into contact with structure (ie: points or sandbars) they tend to break all at once or "close out".

sets- Groups of relatively larger waves traveling together.

lulls- The calm periods in between sets.

wetsuit numbering system- Indicates the thickness, in millimeters, of different panels on the suit. Ex: **5-4-3** means 5mm in the torso, 4mm in the legs, and 3mm in the arms.

inside- Area between the breaking waves and the beach.

outside- Area seaward of the breakers.

rips- Zones or channels in the beach or reef where water flows back out to sea.

duck-dive- Technique for diving under incoming waves with a surfboard.

Types of Waves \ Breaks

point- Rocky or sandy headlands or notches in the coastline where waves strike and break in a constant direction. ex: Seaside

reef- A rocky submerged structure that waves strike and break in a consistent direction. ex: Boiler Bay

protected beach- Stretch of beach that has some kind of structure, man-made or natural, such as jetties or headlands protecting it from wind and or swell. ex: Pacific City

exposed beach- Stretch of beach with no protection structures, "wide open" to wind and swell. ex: Nesika Beach.

bay or river wave- Break where the swell has traveled inside and is breaking in the bay or river rather than the ocean. ex: Florence \ Siuslaw River.

Wave Power Classes

mushy- Gentle \ gradual sloping waves, ideal for beginners and longboards.

fun- Steeper, semi-hollow, shortboardable waves.

juicy- Hollow, powerful waves. Not for beginners.

explosive- Super hollow, scary powerful, and dangerous. Experienced surfers only.

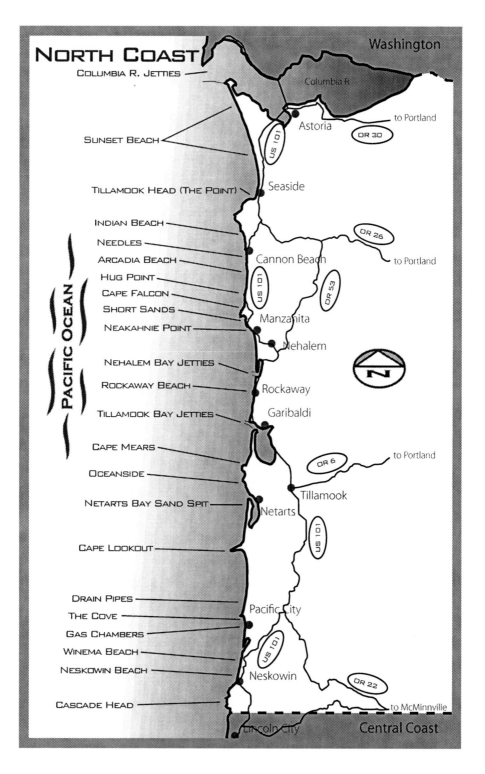

NORTH COAST

Washington

COLUMBIA R. JETTIES

Columbia R.

to Portland

Astoria

OR 30

US 101

SUNSET BEACH

TILLAMOOK HEAD (THE POINT)

Seaside

INDIAN BEACH

OR 26

NEEDLES

to Portland

ARCADIA BEACH

Cannon Beach

HUG POINT

CAPE FALCON

US 101

OR 53

SHORT SANDS

Manzanita

NEAKAHNIE POINT

Nehalem

NEHALEM BAY JETTIES

ROCKAWAY BEACH

Rockaway

TILLAMOOK BAY JETTIES

Garibaldi

CAPE MEARS

OCEANSIDE

OR 6

to Portland

NETARTS BAY SAND SPIT

Tillamook

Netarts

US 101

CAPE LOOKOUT

DRAIN PIPES

THE COVE

Pacific City

GAS CHAMBERS

WINEMA BEACH

US 101

NESKOWIN BEACH

Neskowin

OR 22

CASCADE HEAD

to McMinnville

Lincoln City

Central Coast

PACIFIC OCEAN

N

North Coast (Columbia River to Cascade Head)

Columbia River

 Quick Check

> *Type of Wave*: river mouth
> *Power*: juicy
> *Swell Size and Direction*: all swells over 8ft
> *Wind Direction*: East, light winds
> *Tide*: slack or incoming tides
> *Crowd Factor*: empty
> *Access*: via Fort Stephens
> *Hazards*: You name it, current, sharks and freighters top the list.
> *Vibe*: mellow

Notes: This spot is not normally surfed (and shouldn't be without intimate river knowledge), though it does have its day. Large waves break over river bars. Usually too confused to consider for a surf.

Clatsop Spit (South Jetty Columbia R.)

 Quick Check

> *Type of Wave*: protected beach
> *Power*: fun to juicy
> *Swell Size and Direction*: all swells under 10ft
> *Wind Direction*: North to East
> *Tide*: mid to high, incoming
> *Crowd Factor*: empty
> *Access*: Through Fort Stevens State Park (fort day use area, not the campground), follow signs to Columbia River (approx. 4 miles) then parking area "C" to access the jetty area.
> *Hazards*: rocks, rips, sharks, etc…
> *Vibe*: mellow

Notes: Good looking beach that's tricky to find, use your Delorme map.

© Botkins

SUNSET BEACH (CLATSOP SPIT TO TILLAMOOK HEAD)

Quick Check

Type of Wave: exposed beach
Power: fun to juicy
Swell Size and Direction: all swells under 8ft
Wind Direction: East, light winds
Tide: mid to high, incoming
Crowd Factor: empty, but a few surfers as you go South towards Seaside
Access: side roads off Hwy 101
Hazards: rips, sharks, etc...
Vibe: usually glad to see someone else out

Notes: A lot of nice houses in the area, plenty of beach access and parking.

SEASIDE TILLAMOOK HEAD (AKA THE POINT, THE COVE)

 Quick Check

Type of Wave: point (left) \ protected beach

Power: fun to explosive

Swell Size and Direction: groundswells 5ft or larger for "The Point", best on straight Wests or Southwests. "The Cove" can be surfed on above mentioned and smaller swells as well.

Wind Direction: East to South, light winds

Tide: all tides, gets weak on higher tides

Crowd Factor: just a couple to crowded

Access: Parking all along the cove on Ocean Vista Dr., hike out the rocks to the point or hop right into the rip to surf the cove.

Hazards: super slippery rocks, rips, sharks, etc…

Vibe: aggressive locals

<u>Notes</u>: Two spots here: 1) **The Point** (Tillamook Head). Arguably the best, most consistant wave in Oregon, possibly the Northwest. Two points actually, neither of which are for beginners. Second point which is closer to the cove, is the main attraction. It's a classic and powerful left hand point that leaves a lasting impression on one's psyche, an infamous wave not only for its power but for the locals who frequent and defend it. Remember respect is a two way street and you'll be fine. First point is further out to sea, bigger, messier and much less surfed.2) **The Cove**. A large and powerful rip currents runs along the rocks and out towards the point creating a deep channel that separates the beach from the point. This creates easy access not only to the point but also to the beach break just to the North. This spot does get excellent and is more suitable for beginners.

ECOLA STATE PARK (AKA INDIAN BEACH)

 Quick Check

Type of Wave: protected beach

Power: mushy to fun

Swell Size and Direction: all swells under 8ft

Wind Direction: North to East, light winds

Tide: mid to high, incoming

Crowd Factor: crowded

Access: Enter through Ecola State Park on the North end of Cannon Beach, pay $3 entrance fee at the gate and park in the Indian Beach lot, short hike to the beach.

Hazards: rocks, rips, sharks, etc…

Vibe: mostly beginners here, mellow

<u>Notes</u>: Can get good on peaky summer swells, bigger groundswells start to close out. Great beginner spot.

CANNON BEACH AREA

 Quick Check

Type of Wave: exposed beach
Power: fun to juicy
Swell Size and Direction: all swells under 8ft
Wind Direction: East, light winds
Tide: mid to high, incoming (except low tide for Needles)
Crowd Factor: just a couple
Access: Public access abounds in town, summer weekends can be crowded.
Hazards: rocks, rips, sharks, etc…
Vibe: mellow

Notes: Lots of beach break in town (good parking at Tolavana Beach on the South end of town), most commonly surfed spot is called "Needles", just South of Haystack Rock.

ARCADIA BEACH

 Quick Check

Type of Wave: exposed beach
Power: fun to juicy
Swell Size and Direction: all swells under 8ft
Wind Direction: East, light winds
Tide: mid to high, incoming
Crowd Factor: just a couple
Access: parking in Arcadia Beach State Wayside lot at 101 MP 32.5
Hazards: rocks, rips, sharks, etc…
Vibe: mellow

Notes: Occasionally good rights and lefts, lots of current, hard to get out when the swell is over 5ft.

HUG POINT

 Quick Check

Type of Wave: exposed beach
Power: fun to juicy
Swell Size and Direction: all swells under 8ft
Wind Direction: East, light winds
Tide: mid to high, incoming
Crowd Factor: empty
Access: Parking in Hug Point State Wayside lot at 101 MP 33.5.
Hazards: rocks, rips, sharks, etc…
Vibe: mellow

Notes: Rarely surfed, lots of potential, similar conditions and set up as Arcadia.

CAPE FALCON AREA

 Quick Check

Type of Wave: exposed beach, protected beach, reef
Power: mushy \ beginner to juicy
Swell Size and Direction: all swells under 8ft
Wind Direction: East, light winds
Tide: mid to high, incoming
Crowd Factor: empty
Access: turn off at about 101 MP 36 at Falcon Cove Rd.
Hazards: rocks, rips, sharks, etc…
Vibe: happy to see someone

Notes: Rarely surfed, a lot of potential.

OSWALD WEST STATE PARK (AKA SHORT SANDS, SHORTIES, SMUGGLERS COVE)

 Quick Check

Type of Wave: protected beach
Power: mushy \ beginner to fun
Swell Size and Direction: all swells under 10ft
Wind Direction: East to Northwest, light winds
Tide: mid to high, incoming
Crowd Factor: ultra crowded
Access: Two parking lots around 101 MP 39.5, ten minute hike to the beach.
Hazards: rocks, rips, sharks, etc…
Vibe: too crowded to care

Notes: Maybe the most crowded spot in Oregon. Beautiful hike and beach, very protected and relatively warm. Summer North winds blow offshore and bigger South swells show quite nicely. Longer interval swells start to wall up and close out here. Depending on sand bar quality, it can get quite good, mostly fast peaky lefts up and down the sandy cove. Very strong rip on the South end provides easy access on bigger days. Extremely crowded but sometimes it's the only option on the North coast when you just gotta surf.

NEAKAHNIE MOUNTAIN \ POINT
Quick Check
Type of Wave: point, protected beach
Power: fun to juicy
Swell Size and Direction: groundswells 6 to 10ft
Wind Direction: North to East, light winds
Tide: low, incoming
Crowd Factor: just a couple
Access: via the small town of Manzanita
Hazards: slippery rocks, rips, sharks, etc…
Vibe: Mellow, show respect, this place has a following.

Notes: Check this spot from several cliffside overlooks on 101 around MP 41. Quality yet fickle waves, careful on the rocks getting in and out. Lots of quality beach break to the South in and around town.

© Botkins

NEHALEM BAY JETTIES
Quick Check
Type of Wave: exposed beach, protected beach
Power: fun to juicy
Swell Size and Direction: all swells under 8ft
Wind Direction: North to East, light winds
Tide: low to mid, incoming
Crowd Factor: empty to just a couple
Access: Turn off 101 at MP 48.8 onto Beach St., then head North about a mile to the South jetty.
Hazards: rocks, rips, sharks, etc…
Vibe: mellow

Notes: Jetties on the North and South side of the river provide shelter from the winds, lots of potential, rarely surfed.

ROCKAWAY BEACH

 Quick Check

Type of Wave: exposed beach
Power: fun to juicy
Swell Size and Direction: all swells under 8ft
Wind Direction: East, light winds
Tide: low to mid, incoming
Crowd Factor: empty
Access: plenty of public access points in town
Hazards: rips, sharks, etc…
Vibe: mellow

Notes: About 4 miles of lonely beach break between Nehalem and Tillamook bays, rarely surfed.

© Botkins

TILLAMOOK BAY JETTIES (AKA BAR VIEW)

Quick Check

Type of Wave: protected beach
Power: fun to juicy
Swell Size and Direction: all swells under 10ft
Wind Direction: all directions except West
Tide: all tides
Crowd Factor: just a couple
Access: Access the North jetty via Barview County Park at 101 MP 54.0
(Cedar Ave.) To access the South jetty drive \ hike out Bayocean
Dike Rd or by paddling across the bay! Not for the inexperienced.
Hazards: rocks, rips, sharks, etc…
Vibe: Show respect and you'll receive it. Don't expect a welcoming committee.

Notes: Both of these spots are regularly surfed, but can be considered fickle. The North jetty wave breaks way out there, and is spooky. Not a beginner spot!

CAPE MEARS

Quick Check

Type of Wave: protected beach
Power: fun to juicy
Swell Size and Direction: all swells under 8ft
Wind Direction: South to East, light winds
Tide: low to mid, incoming
Crowd Factor: empty
Access: Bayocean Rd. from Tillamook to the village of Cape Mears,
        plenty of parking.
Hazards: rocks, rips, sharks, etc…
Vibe: mellow

Notes: Large rocky headland provides some protection from South winds. Worth a look, rarely surfed.

© Botkins

OCEANSIDE

Quick Check

Type of Wave: protected beach
Power: fun to juicy
Swell Size and Direction: all swells under 8ft
Wind Direction: East, light winds, far North end of cove protected from
        North winds
Tide: low to mid, incoming
Crowd Factor: empty to just a couple
Access: Plenty of public parking in the town of Oceanside.
Hazards: rocks, rips, sharks, etc…
Vibe: mellow

Notes: It does get good here, just not that often. This beach typically has strong long-shore currents.

Quick Check

Type of Wave: exposed beach
Power: fun to juicy
Swell Size and Direction: all swells under 8ft
Wind Direction: East, light winds
Tide: low to mid, incoming
Crowd Factor: empty to just a couple
Access: via Cape Lookout State Park
Hazards: rips, sharks, etc…
Vibe: mellow

Notes: Heading South on Cape Lookout Rd., past the state park, when the roads starts to gain elevation, there's a nice viewpoint pullout. Check the beach from here and find your peak.

© Cove Photo

CAPE LOOKOUT (AKA THE CAMP)

Quick Check

Type of Wave: point \ reef (right)
Power: fun to juicy
Swell Size and Direction: West to Southwest groundswells, 5 to 10ft
Wind Direction: East to North, light winds
Tide: mid
Crowd Factor: Can get crowded, usually just a few.
Access: Park at trailhead at the peak of Cape Lookout Rd., hike about 2 miles down to the beach on the South side of the cape. Also you can access the beach via Sand Lake Off-Road Use Area.
Hazards: rocks, rips, sharks, etc…
Vibe: Locals here aren't stoked to have visitors, show respect.

Notes: Classic Oregon wave, great when its on but can be fickle. Beach break to the South of the point can produce quality surf to.

PACIFIC CITY AREA

 Quick Check

Type of Wave: exposed beach, protected beach
Power: mushy \ beginner to juicy
Swell Size and Direction: all swells under 8ft
Wind Direction: East to North, light winds
Tide: all
Crowd Factor: just a couple to mega crowded
Access: Get to Pacific City via Sand Lake Rd. and the Three Capes
Scenic Loop. Access to surf is everywhere, see notes.
Hazards: rocks, rips, sharks, etc...
Vibe: Mellow, how could you be agro with that many people, its over the top.

Notes: This Area is extremely popular with weekenders and out of area surfers, for good reason because it gets downright good surf. There are three main surf areas around town.

1) The North side of Cape Kiwanda ("Drainpipes"): lonely beach break, little or no wind protection but catches tons of swell. Go here on small, calm days. Access along Cape Dr.

2) The South side of the cape ("The Cove"): a quazi right point wave at times adjacent to the rocks on the North end of the cove, very sand dependent. As you go South in the cove ("Gas Chambers"), right in front of the big rock (Haystack Rock) there are usually some good sandbars. Huge day use parking lot on the North end of town, impossible to miss.

3) The South end of the beach: continuing South towards Bob Straub State Park and the Nestucca River mouth, more quality beach breaks that pick up more swell and are less crowded.

Pacific City gets great summer conditions and is a fun place to surf and hang. The Pelican Pub is right in the parking lot for "The Cove", nice place to have a beer and watch the circus.

WINEMA BEACH

 Quick Check

Type of Wave: exposed beach
Power: fun to juicy
Swell Size and Direction: all swells under 8ft
Wind Direction: East, light winds
Tide: mid to high, incoming
Crowd Factor: empty
Access: via Winema Rd. at 101 MP 93.75
Hazards: rips, sharks, etc...
Vibe: mellow

Notes: More quality beach break, rarely surfed. There's a nice viewpoint pullout at 101 MP 94.25 for a check.

NESKOWIN

 Quick Check

Type of Wave: exposed beach
Power: fun to juicy
Swell Size and Direction: all swells under 8ft
Wind Direction: East, light winds
Tide: low to mid, incoming
Crowd Factor: empty
Access: Plenty of public access in town
Hazards: rocks, rips, sharks, etc…
Vibe: mellow
Notes: Rarely surfed, worth a look.

© DoubleVizion

CASCADE HEAD \ SALMON RIVER

 Quick Check

Type of Wave: protected beach
Power: fun to juicy
Swell Size and Direction: all swells under 8ft
Wind Direction: North to East, light winds
Tide: all, incoming
Crowd Factor: empty
Access: Tricky, turn off 101 at MP 104 onto Three Rocks Rd. for about 2
 miles to boat ramp. Paddle across the river and hike out to
 the beach.
Hazards: rocks, rips, sharks, etc…
Vibe: mellow
Notes: Almost never surfed but worth the effort. Pretty sharky, the Salmon River
has a very healthy early fall run.

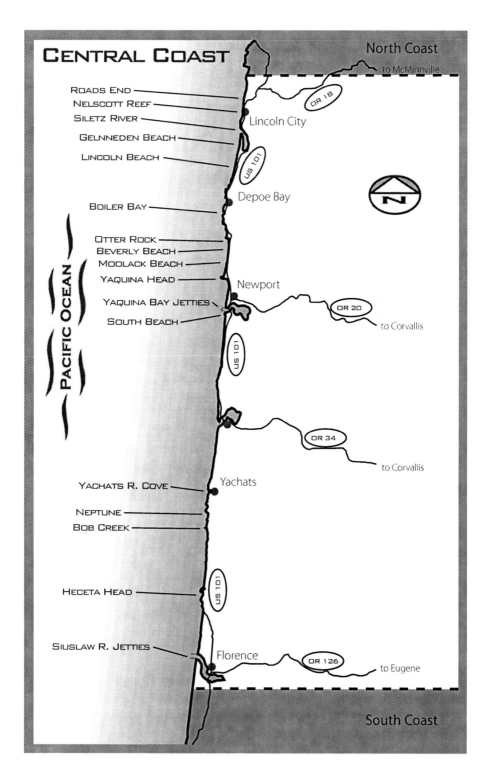

CENTRAL COAST

ROADS END
NELSCOTT REEF
SILETZ RIVER
GELUNNEDEN BEACH
LINCOLN BEACH

Lincoln City

OR 18

US 101

Depoe Bay

N

BOILER BAY

OTTER ROCK
BEVERLY BEACH
MOOLACK BEACH
YAQUINA HEAD
YAQUINA BAY JETTIES
SOUTH BEACH

Newport

OR 20

to Corvallis

PACIFIC OCEAN

US 101

OR 34

to Corvallis

YACHATS R. COVE

Yachats

NEPTUNE
BOB CREEK

HECETA HEAD

US 101

SIUSLAW R. JETTIES

Florence

OR 126

to Eugene

South Coast

Central Coast (Cascade Head to Florence)

Lincoln City Area (Roads End to Siletz River)

 Quick Check

Type of Wave: exposed beach, protected beach, reef

Power: mushy \ beginner to juicy

Swell Size and Direction: all swells under 10ft (except "Canyons" see below)

Wind Direction: East, light winds

Tide: all

Crowd Factor: empty to just a couple

Access: Most notable access at Roads End State Wayside on the North end of town and the D River State Wayside in mid town. Small access lots are everywhere throughout town, parking is not a problem.

Hazards: rocks, rips, sharks, etc...

Vibe: mellow

Notes: About 7 miles of beach break that can produce some quality surf. Mostly unremarkable except for an offshore reef in the Nelscott area of town. Nelscott Reef (aka "Canyons") is Oregon's most publicized big wave tow-in spot and is starting to get a following, including a contest. Fun to watch for most of us. Go here on BIG winter groundswells over 10ft. For more contest info go to www. nelscottreef.com.

Glenneden and Lincoln Beach

 Quick Check

Type of Wave: exposed beach

Power: juicy

Swell Size and Direction: all swells under 6ft

Wind Direction: East, light

Tide: all, changes a lot with tide

Crowd Factor: just a couple

Access: Parking on most residential streets is fine, little trails down to the beach are numerous.

Hazards: rips, sharks, etc...

Vibe: mellow

Notes: Unique Northwest facing deepwater beach break. About 6 miles of beach from Glenneden Sand Spit (Siletz River Mouth) South to Fisherman's Rock. Steep beach and deepwater close to shore makes for very powerful peaky waves, not for beginners.

BOILER BAY

 Quick Check

Type of Wave: reef (right)
Power: juicy to explosive
Swell Size and Direction: all swells over 6ft
Wind Direction: South to East, light winds
Tide: low to mid
Crowd Factor: empty to semi-crowded
Access: Parking at Boiler Bay State Scenic Viewpoint at 101 MP 125
      (1 mile North of Depoe Bay).
Hazards: rocks, urchins, rips, sharks, etc…
Vibe: Don't expect a welcoming committee.

Notes: Semi-sketchy right hand reef breaks hollow directly off a little rock finger. In the Northwest corner of the bay is Scott's Reef, an ultra-heavy surge reef, very fun to watch and photograph, needs a solid swell to show.

© Botkins

OTTER ROCK (AKA DEVILÍS PUNCHBOWL)

 Quick Check

Type of Wave: protected beach
Power: mushy \ beginner to fun
Swell Size and Direction: all swells under 8ft, really likes Souths
Wind Direction: North to East, light winds
Tide: all
Crowd Factor: ultra-crowded
Access: Turn off at 101 MP's 131.5 or 133 to get to parking lot at Devil's Punchbowl State Natural Area, then take the steps down to the beach.
Hazards: rocks, rips, sharks, etc…
Vibe: mellow

Notes: Beautiful and warm protected sandy cove, one of the most popular spots on the Central coast. Surf can get good although it's generally weak and small, great beginner spot. As you go South from the cove towards Beverly Beach it generally gets bigger and more exposed to the wind.

BEVERLY BEACH

 Quick Check

    Type of Wave: exposed beach
    Power: fun to juicy
    Swell Size and Direction: all swells under 8ft
    Wind Direction: East, light winds
    Tide: mid to high, incoming
    Crowd Factor: just a couple
    Access: Pullouts along 101 and via Beverley Beach State Park at MP 134.
    Hazards: rocks, rips, sharks, etc…
    Vibe: mellow

Notes: Some offshore islands and rocks keep this place a bit smaller than the more exposed beach just South (Moolack Beach). Can get good and is surfed quite regularly.

© DoubleVizion

MOOLACK BEACH

 Quick Check

    Type of Wave: exposed beach
    Power: fun to juicy
    Swell Size and Direction: all swells under 8ft
    Wind Direction: East, light winds
    Tide: mid to high, incoming
    Crowd Factor: just a couple
    Access: pullouts along 101 around MP 136
    Hazards: rocks, rips, sharks, etc…
    Vibe: mellow

Notes: More exposed and bigger than Beverley Beach, surfed just as regularly with similar quality. This place is always bigger than it looks from up on the highway.

AGATE BEACH (YAQUINA HEAD)

 Quick Check

Type of Wave: point \ protected beach
Power: mushy \ beginner to juicy
Swell Size and Direction: All swells under 8ft, except groundswells over
      8ft for "Avalanche"
Wind Direction: North to East, light winds
Tide: all
Crowd Factor: crowded
Access: Large lot on 101 at MP 137.75, just South of the light for 52nd St.
      Walk to the beach.
Hazards: rocks, rips, sharks, etc…
Vibe: mellow to agro at times

Notes: A very popular spot with beginners and long boarders, summer North wind is offshore here. Mostly rights depending on the sand bars. Solid groundswells break on the outer bar producing quality large waves (aka "Avalanche").

SOUTH BEACH (NEWPORT)

 Quick Check

Type of Wave: protected beach
Power: fun to juicy
Swell Size and Direction: all swells under 8ft
Wind Direction: North to East, light winds
Tide: all
Crowd Factor: semi-crowded
Access: Via South Jetty Rd. just South of the bridge (take Aquarium exit)
      and South Beach State Park at 101 MP 143.25
Hazards: rips, sharks, etc…
Vibe: grumpy locals

Notes: South Jetty of Yaquina Bay provides wind and swell protection. Depending on sand bars, quality surf can be found. Very fickle and punishing, waves usually break pretty far out with a lot of power. Mostly lefts. Popular with windsurfers and kiters.

SOUTH BEACH TO WALDPORT BEACHES

 Quick Check

Type of Wave: exposed beach
Power: fun to juicy
Swell Size and Direction: all swells under 8ft
Wind Direction: East, light winds
Tide: all
Crowd Factor: empty
Access: pullouts along 101
Hazards: rocks, rips, sharks, etc...
Vibe: mellow

Notes: Unremarkable beach break with rocks here and there, rarely surfed. The highway is within site of the ocean for most of this stretch with plenty of little access points.

YACHATS

 Quick Check

Type of Wave: semi-protected rocky beaches (that about covers it)
Power: mushy \ beginner to juicy
Swell Size and Direction: all swells under 8ft
Wind Direction: East, light winds
Tide: all
Crowd Factor: empty
Access: Yachats State Park on the North side of the river or turn onto Yachats Ocean Rd. just South of the river bridge to access the South side.
Hazards: rocks, rips, sharks, etc...
Vibe: mellow

Notes: The Yachats River empties into a sandy \ rocky cove, quality waves can be found here when the planets align.

NEPTUNE

 Quick Check

Type of Wave: semi-protected rocky beach
Power: fun to juicy
Swell Size and Direction: all swells under 8ft
Wind Direction: North to East, light winds
Tide: all
Crowd Factor: empty
Access: Neptune State Scenic Viewpoint at 101 MP 168.25.
Hazards: rocks, rips, sharks, etc…
Vibe: mellow

Notes: Rarely surfed, inviting little cove with a lot of potential.

© Botkins

BOB CREEK

 Quick Check

Type of Wave: reef (right)
Power: juicy to explosive
Swell Size and Direction: all swells under 8ft
Wind Direction: East, light winds
Tide: mid
Crowd Factor: empty to just a couple
Access: Parking at Bob Creek State Scenic Viewpoint at 101 MP 170.
Hazards: rocks, rips, sharks, lots of current and deceptive power
Vibe: mellow to semi-agro

Notes: Sandy and rocky cove with reef on the outside. Regulary surfed and a bit legendary with its potential and history. Very hollow and fast right hand wave.

HECETA HEAD (AKA DEVILíS ELBOW)

 Quick Check

Type of Wave: protected beach
Power: mushy \ beginner to juicy
Swell Size and Direction: all swells under 10ft
Wind Direction: North to East, light winds
Tide: mid to high, incoming
Crowd Factor: empty to just a couple
Access: Parking at Heceta Head Lighthouse State Scenic Viewpoint at
      101 MP 178.2.
Hazards: rocks, rips, sharks, etc…
Vibe: mellow

Notes: Very picturesque little sandy cove, lots of potential but rarely surfed.

FLORENCE AREA (SIUSLAW RIVER JETTIES)

 Quick Check

Type of Wave: protected beach, river wave
Power: mushy \ beginner to juicy
Swell Size and Direction: all swells under 10ft (except in river, bigger
      swells are surfable)
Wind Direction: all directions
Tide: all, incoming in the river
Crowd Factor: just a couple to semi-crowded
Access: The North jetty via Heceta Beach Rd. at 101 MP 187.2, then
      Rhododendron Dr. and North Jetty Rd. or just follow the signs to
      Harbor Vista County Park. For the South jetty turn off 101 at
      MP 191.8 at the Oregon Dunes National Recreation Area, then
      head North and West for 6 miles to the jetty and Southern beach.
      Most people access the river wave via the South jetty area.
Hazards: rocks, rips, sharks, river current
Vibe: mellow to semi-agro

Notes: River wave breaks right off the South jetty about a half-mile upstream
from the mouth, can get good depending on the state of the dredged channel.
Surf the incoming or slack tide only, water is extra cold! The South beach is
typical jetty beach break, lots of potential and regularly surfed. Popular with
windsurfers and kiters. Extra Note: You don't need to pay at the gate if you are
only going to the jetty, which is a US Army Corp of Engineers site and separate
from the Dunes Facility.

One Last Note: From about 10 miles North of Florence South to Winchester Bay is windy "dune country", approximately 40 miles of wide open beach break with little variation but none-the-less lots of potential for quality surf.

© DoubleVizion

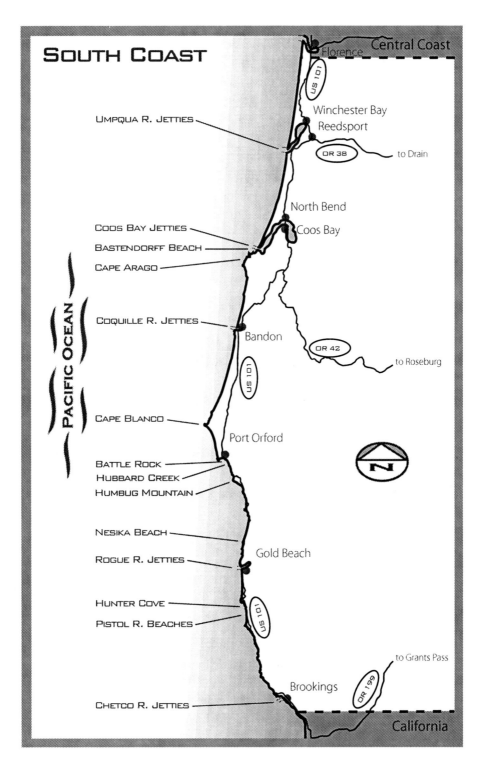

SOUTH COAST

PACIFIC OCEAN

Central Coast
Florence
US 101
Winchester Bay
Reedsport
UMPQUA R. JETTIES
OR 38 — to Drain

North Bend
COOS BAY JETTIES — Coos Bay
BASTENDORFF BEACH
CAPE ARAGO

COQUILLE R. JETTIES
Bandon
OR 42 — to Roseburg
US 101

CAPE BLANCO
Port Orford
BATTLE ROCK
HUBBARD CREEK
HUMBUG MOUNTAIN

N

NESIKA BEACH
ROGUE R. JETTIES — Gold Beach

HUNTER COVE
PISTOL R. BEACHES
US 101

to Grants Pass
OR 199
Brookings
CHETCO R. JETTIES
California

SOUTH COAST (FLORENCE TO THE CALIFORNIA BORDER)

WINCHESTER BAY (UMPQUA RIVER JETTIES)

 Quick Check

Type of Wave: protected beach
Power: fun to juicy
Swell Size and Direction: all swells under 10ft
Wind Direction: North to East, light winds
Tide: all
Crowd Factor: just a couple to semi-crowded
Access: For the South jetty turn West off 101 at MP 215.75 at Salmon
Harbor Dr. then follow signs about 2 miles to the beach. The
North jetty has no easy access, either boat, paddle, or ATV in,
rarely to never surfed.
Hazards: rocks, rips, sharks, etc...
Vibe: mellow to semi-agro

Notes: Powerful peaky waves, not a beginner spot. South of here for about 35
miles is more dune country, very hard access to wide open beach break. I'm sure
it gets good with no one there to see it.

CAPE ARAGO \ BASTENDORFF BEACH

 Quick Check

Type of Wave: protected beach, reef
Power: mushy \ beginner to juicy
Swell Size and Direction: all swells under 12ft
Wind Direction: all directions
Tide: all
Crowd Factor: just a couple
Access: Turn off 101 at MP 236 (Virginia Blvd.) and follow signs to
Charlestown then the beach, 11 miles off the highway.
Hazards: rocks, rips, sharks, etc...
Vibe: mellow to semi-agro

Notes: Bastendorff Beach is the most commonly surfed spot in this stretch, a
rare Northwest facing beach break. Tons of potential spots to the South out to
the point proper. Cape Arago is a very scenic area worth the drive just to see it
regardless of the surf.

BANDON (COQUILLE RIVER JETTIES)

 Quick Check

Type of Wave: protected beach
Power: fun to juicy
Swell Size and Direction: all swells under 8ft
Wind Direction: South and North to East, light winds
Tide: all
Crowd Factor: just a couple
Access: Turn West at 101 MP 263.25, go through Old Town Bandon
 and follow signs to South Jetty County Park. For the North jetty
 turn off 101 at MP 259 at the Bollards Beach State Park turn and
 follow signs to Coquille River Light.
Hazards: rocks, rips, sharks, etc…
Vibe: mellow
Notes: Typical South jetty wave, plenty of power. North side is very rarely surfed.

© Cove Photo

CAPE BLANCO

 Quick Check

Type of Wave: protected beach, reef
Power: mushy \ beginner to juicy
Swell Size and Direction: all swells under 12ft
Wind Direction: all directions except West
Tide: all
Crowd Factor: just a couple
Access: Via Cape Blanco State Park, turnoff at 101 MP 296.5, go past
 the camping area about 1 mile to the lighthouse day use area.
Hazards: rocks, rips, sharks, etc…
Vibe: mellow
Notes: There are coves on the North and South sides of the point, both offer
wind protection and quality surf. Mostly beach but some outer reefs can produce
as well. This is one of the windiest places on the Oregon coast (most Westerly
point in Oregon), feels like you're on the moon.

PORT ORFORD AREA

 Quick Check

Type of Wave: semi-protected beaches, reef
Power: mushy \ beginner to juicy
Swell Size and Direction: All swells up to 15 ft, big Northwest swells
      can be surfable in this area.
Wind Direction: North to East, light winds
Tide: all
Crowd Factor: just a couple to semi-crowded
Access: Battle Rock State Wayside at 101 MP 301.25 and Hubbard
Creek via a pullout at 101 MP 302.25
Hazards: rocks, rips, sharks, etc…
Vibe: mellow

Notes: The South facing beaches from Battle Rock South to Hubbard Creek are regularly surfed. North winds howl offshore here.

© Cove Photo

HUMBUG MOUNTAIN STATE PARK

 Quick Check

Type of Wave: semi-protected beach
Power: mushy \ beginner to juicy
Swell Size and Direction: all swells under 12ft
Wind Direction: North to East, light winds
Tide: mid to high
Crowd Factor: empty to just a couple
Access: Via Humbug Mountain State Park at 101 MP 307.
Hazards: rocks, rips, sharks, etc…
Vibe: mellow

Notes: Sand and rock cove West of the campground. You get a glimpse of the cove from the highway at about 101 MP 306.

NESIKA BEACH

 Quick Check

Type of Wave: exposed beach
Power: fun to juicy
Swell Size and Direction: all swells under 8ft
Wind Direction: East, light winds
Tide: mid to high, incoming
Crowd Factor: empty
Access: Visible along 101 with pullouts at MP 317 through about 321.
Hazards: rips, sharks, etc…
Vibe: mellow

Notes: Wide open and very powerful beach break.

GOLD BEACH (ROGUE RIVER JETTIES)

 Quick Check

Type of Wave: protected beach, river wave
Power: mushy \ beginner to juicy
Swell Size and Direction: all swells under 8ft
Wind Direction: all directions except West
Tide: all, incoming in the river
Crowd Factor: just a couple
Access: For the North jetty turn off 101 at MP 326.5 on the Old Coast
Road and head South then West for about 1 mile to the jetty. For
the South jetty turn off 101 at MP 328.5 on Port Dr. and follow
signs for about a mile again.
Hazards: rocks, rips, river current, boats, sharks, etc…
Vibe: mellow

Notes: The North and South jetties both produce quality surf and are regularly surfed. Inside the jetties is a sandbar that has tons of potential but rarely comes alive.

HUNTER COVE

 Quick Check

Type of Wave: protected beach, point (right)
Power: mushy \ beginner to juicy
Swell Size and Direction: all swells under 12ft
Wind Direction: North to East, light winds
Tide: all
Crowd Factor: empty to crowded
Access: Pullout on 101 at MP 336.5, then hike North up the beach to the cove.
Hazards: rocks, rips, sharks, etc...
Vibe: mellow to agro

Notes: Sandy protected cove. Can produce quality surf, has had periods of popularity in the past. Beaches leading South out of the cove in the vicinity of the Pistol River are also worth a look, very popular with windsurfers and kiters.

* **NOTE**: Between Hunter Cove and Brookings are about 25 miles of wild and scenic coastline, bring your binoculars and hiking boots and you will be rewarded, maybe.

BROOKINGS AREA (CHETCO RIVER JETTIES)

 Quick Check

Type of Wave: protected beach, reef
Power: mushy \ beginner to juicy
Swell Size and Direction: all swells under 10ft
Wind Direction: all directions except West
Tide: all
Crowd Factor: empty to semi-crowded
Access: For the South jetty turn off 101 at MP 358 (South Bank Road) and follow signs.
Hazards: rocks, rips, sharks, etc...
Vibe: mellow

Notes: There is some surf around town in addition to the jetties. The Brookings area is in a little "Banana Belt" and gets unusually warm and pleasant weather for the Oregon coast, you may find yourself thinking you're much further South than you actually are.

OK Now What?

So you've traveled the coast and are sitting on the California border considering your options, as far as I can see you have two. 1) Continue South and explore the Northern Cali scene, which surely can produce quality surf and experiences or...2) Head North and find all the spots I didn't even hint of in this guide.

What a dilemma! Good luck and play nice.

SURF SHOPS

NORTH COAST

(**Note**: This list may not be comprehensive or up to date as new shops seem to sprout up on a daily basis.)

WASHINGTON

Pacific Wave Ltd. www.pacwave.net
21 Highway 101
Warrenton, WA, 97146 888.223.9794

SEASIDE & ASTORIA

Cold Water Surf Shop www.coldwatersurf.com
1126 Marine Dr.
Astoria, OR, 97103 503.325.3294

Seaside Sur f Shop www.seadsidesurfshop.com
1116 S. Rosevelt (101)
Seaside, OR, 97138 503.717.1110

Cleanline Surf Co. www.cleanlinesurf.com
719 1st Ave.
Seaside, OR, 97138 503.738.7888

CANNON BEACH

Cleanline Surf Co. www.cleanlinesurf.com
171 Sunset Blvd.
Cannon Beach, OR, 97110 503.436.9726

Cannon Beach Surf Shop www.cannonbeachsurf.com
2 locations
1088 S. Hemlock 503.436.0475
240 N. Hemlock 503.436.0479
Cannon Beach, OR, 97110

PACIFIC CITY

South County Surf Shop
33310 Cape Kiwanda Dr.
Pacific City, OR, 97135

Kiwanda Surf Shop www.kiwandasurfco.com
6305 Pacific Ave.
Pacific City, OR, 97135 503.965.3627

Central Coast

Lincoln City

Safari Town Surf Shop
3026 NE Hwy 101
Lincoln City, OR, 97367 541.996.6335

Lincoln City Surf Shop www.lcsurfshop.com
4792 SE Hwy 101
Lincoln City, OR, 97367 541.996.7433

Oregon Surf Shop www.oregonsurfshop.com
4933 SW Hwy 101
Lincoln City, OR, 97367 541.996.3957, 877.339.5672

Nelscott Reef Surf Shop www.nelscottreef.com
1800 SE Hwy 101, #E
Lincoln City, OR, 97367 541.996.6122

Depoe Bay

Otter Rock Surf Shop www.otterrocksurf.com
488 N. Hwy 101
Depoe Bay, OR, 97341 541.765.2776

Newport

Ossies Surf Shop www.ossiessurfshop.com
4860 N. Coast Hwy
Newport, OR 97365 541.574.4634

Ocean Pulse Surf Shop
429 SW N. Coast Hwy
Newport, OR, 97365 541.265.7745

South Coast

Coos Bay

Rocky Point Surf & Sport
222 S. Broadway
Coos Bay, OR, 97420 541.888.9370

Waxer's Surf & Skate
222 S. Broadway
Coos Bay, OR, 97420 541.348.2213

Northwest Surf Shop 541.756.5792

PORT ORFORD

Pop's Surf Shop
428 9th St.
Port Orford, OR, 97465 541.332.0822

BROOKINGS

Sessions Surf Shop www.sessionsurf.com
800 Chetco Rd. (Hwy 101)
Brookings, OR, 97415 541.412.0810

INLAND SHOPS

PORTLAND

Gorge Performance www.gorgeperformance.com
7400 Macadam Ave.
Portland, OR, 97219 503.246.6646

All Surf Industry www.allsurfindustry.com
532 SE Clay
Portland, OR, 97214 503.239.8973

HOOD RIVER

Doug's Sports www.dougsports.com
101 Oak St.
Hood River, OR, 97031 541.386.5787

PHILOMATH

Pura Vida Surf Shop www.pvsurfshop.com
1320 Main St..
Philomath, OR, 97370 541.929.7873

EUGENE

Boardsports
265 E. 13th Ave.
Eugene, OR, 97401 541.484.2588

Tactics Board Shop www.tactics.com
375 W. 4th Ave.
Eugene, OR, 97401 541.349.0087 888.450.5060

GRANTS PASS & MEDFORD

Extreme Board Shop www.virtualboardshop.com
2 locations
1661 NE 7th St.
Grants Pass, OR, 97526 541.474.7464
1350 Biddle Rd.
Medford, OR, 97501 541.779.7669

Internet Resources

Waves, Weather, and Water

www.buoyweather.com -small subscription fee for worldwide
  ocean weather forecasting (boating oriented).

www.magicseaweed.com -free worldwide forecasting.

www.nelscottreef.com -Canyons contest info.

http://nwprtsrf.oce.orst.edu -Newport surf report

www.nws.org -National Weather Service, if its about weather, they
  got it.

www.oregonsurf.com -really all you need for your Oregon surfing needs.

www.oregonsurfcheck.com -quick look at forecasts and reports on
  the entire coast.

www.oregonsurfers.com -christian surfers organization.

www.sharkresearchcommittee.com -Pacific Ocean shark research
  and incident reporting.

www.surf-forecast.com free worldwide forecasting.

www.surforecast.com -free North and Central America forecasting.

www.surfline.com -surfing oriented subscription based forecasting
  site. Very extensive site for surfing worldwide, although
  Oregon gets little coverage.

www.surfrider.org -surfer activism and lobby organization.

www.stormsurf.com -free worldwide surf forecasting.

www.wavewatch.com -free worldwide surf forecasting.

www.wannasurf.com -viewer contributed based site concentrates
  on surf spots, they have enough to get you in the water
  anywhere in the world.

www.weather.com -The Weather Channel's website, good detailed
  10-day forecasts, just enter a zip code or town name.

www.wetsand.com -free worldwide surf forecasting.

Oregon Beach Monitoring Program
www.oregon.gov/DHS/ph/beaches/
www.earth911.org/waterquality/

CAMPGROUNDS AND AGENCIES (Note: Only home
pages are listed for government agencies as camping information may
not be all you need. Navigating then, to camground facilities is usually
easy to do.)

Clatsop County -**www.co.clatsop.or.us**

Tillamook County -**www.co.tillamook.or.u**s

Lincoln County -**www.co.lincoln.or.us**

Lane County -**www.co.lane.or.us**

Douglas County -**www.co.douglas.or.us**

Coos County -**www.co.coos.or.us**

Curry County -**www.co.curry.or.us**

State of Oregon -**www.oregon.gov**

Oregon Department of Transportation -**www.odot.state.or.us**

National Forest Service -**www.fs.fed.us**

MAPS
Delorme Gazetteer -all you need.

Printed in the United States
111964LV00004B/264/A